Lessons Learned by a

Patriot Husband and

Dad:

Overcoming Challenges for the Benefit of

Your Family

By LTC (R) Chris Woody

Acknowledgements

As with anything in my life, there has always been someone else involved that made me successful. I have found throughout life that not being the smartest person in the room is absolutely ok. The solution is that you have friends with skills and you always support each other.

I must start out by thanking my Lord and Savior, Jesus Christ. I have made so many mistakes but have also gotten a few things right only because of his grace and mercy.

My terrific and amazing wife Rhonda is next in the batting order. There is not another woman in the world like her or can even come close. She jokingly tells people that she raised five children. Together we have four children and I get to be the fifth child. In all honesty, she had to raise me and tolerate me into maturity. Rhonda, I love you more than the air that I breath!

To my children, Tanner, Rachael, Morgan and Eli. I have never been the perfect dad to you I'm sure but I have loved you from the minute that you were born. You are all so amazing in my eyes. When I was away, you always took it in stride and kept grabbing for life and success. I am so proud of you and thank you so much for still loving me.

Cliff Vicars, you are one amazing man! You and I met while serving as "Black Lions" and you have made an impact on me since then. For those of you reading this, you will see more about Chaplain Vicars in the book. Cliff, I have no way of ever paying you back for investing in my marriage and family without hesitation. I can simply say that I love you like a brother and stand ready to help you whenever and wherever I can.

To my mother-in-law Dianne. I love you like my own mother and owe you a deep debt that I can never repay. Just know that I respect you and honor you. Like this book, you have always been there to help me get my speeches right, fix my messed-up grammar and encouraged me in so many ways. At the end of the day I recognize that you have given me the best thing that you ever had in my eyes. Your beautiful daughter, Rhonda. I will protect her until the day that I die and will spend the rest of my life trying to make her happy.

There are so many friends, family, leaders and peers that have shaped me into who I am. Thank you is simply not enough but know that I stand ready to talk, listen, or help you.

Foreword

The challenges faced by a military husband and father are an enormous task. I write this as a man who has failed in many of the things that we will talk about in this book. The short chapters in this book will hopefully be thought provoking for you as you go throughout your life and career. It is meant to be an easy read and allow you refer back to as you find yourself in some of these situations. This is not a novel that will take a lot of your time because hey, you don't have a lot of time.

Ephesians 5:23-33 (NIV) says

[23] For the husband is the head of the wife as Christ is the head of the church, his body, of which he is the Savior.

[24] Now as the church submits to Christ, so also wives should submit to their husbands in everything.

[25] Husbands, love your wives, just as Christ loved the church and gave himself up for her

[26] to make her holy, cleansing[a] her by the washing with water through the word,

[27] and to present her to himself as a radiant church, without stain or wrinkle or any other blemish, but holy and blameless.

[28] In this same way, husbands ought to love their wives as their own bodies. He who loves his wife loves himself.

[29] After all, no one ever hated their own body, but they feed and care for their body, just as Christ does the church—

[30] for we are members of his body.

[31] "For this reason a man will leave his father and mother and be united to his wife, and the two will become one flesh."[b]

[32] This is a profound mystery—but I am talking about Christ and the church.

[33] However, each one of you also must love his wife as he loves himself, and the wife must respect her husband.

This will be the basis of the issues where we, as men fail but would have saved me a lot of heartache and failure if I had spent more time as a young man understanding my role.

<u>Chapters</u>

Introduction

Let me start by saying that I am nobody special, and this book is not to thump my chest. Rather, it is to share some of my mistakes from 37 years of military service while being a husband and a dad for most of that time. If you are married and/or have children, hopefully you figure out very quickly that they are your number one priority no matter what career field that you take. This doesn't mean that you just stay out of work anytime that you want to take a kid to the doctor or whatever. What it does mean is that you and your wife work together for scheduling and executing family matters. I have learned after 35 years of marriage that anything is possible if you and your wife work together. Let me remind you that you were charged as the head of household by God himself in Ephesians and that brings immense responsibility.

I grew up in a little town called Maiden, North Carolina. Our little town had small farms and lots of textile mills that supported the majority of the families there. If we were poor, we didn't know it. It seems to me that in those days, people were always willing to help each other.

I never knew my real dad (sperm donor) but I was so fortunate to have a Daddy in my life. His name was Will Craig and he fell in love with my mother very early in my life.

He didn't have to love me, but he did. He did love me like I was his own child. I can't say enough about this man that raised me like I was his own son. I never doubted if this man loved me and I never wondered about my real dad. I thought that I had a family that was different than others or weird maybe. There were step brothers and broken marriages all around. Turns out that I honestly was a very lucky kid growing up. I had a mom and dad that really cared about me. We didn't go to church when I was growing up, but I knew that my mother was saved as she told me she was. I wasn't sure about daddy but years later, when he was on his deathbed trying to survive lung cancer, I asked him if he was. He couldn't talk but could nod his head and he told me no. I knew that I only had this one opportunity, so I asked him if he wanted salvation with Jesus and he shook his head yes. With me holding one hand and my nephew Justin holding his other hand, I led him through the prayer of salvation with only his head nods. At some point during the day, I left my wife there with him to go to the store only to get a call to tell me that daddy was gone. I am so thankful for Jesus saving my daddy.

My mom had lived a hard life between just growing up poor and lots of failed relationships. She loved me and worked really hard to show love to everyone. Both mom and dad, worked in textile mills to make ends meet. Daddy worked 1st shift which was from 7am to

3pm and momma worked at another plant on second shift from 3pm to 11pm. We couldn't afford day care, so my mom dropped me off at the guard shack at daddy's mill to hang out with the security guards until daddy got off of his shift then we would go home.

I joined the North Carolina National Guard in 1986 at the ripe old age of 17. I went to Basic Training the summer between my junior and senior years of high school. During my last two years of high school, I worked second shift in the Mill that my dad did. I would get out of school early for having a job and go to work from 3pm to 11pm. If you wanted gas, insurance, or whatever you had to work. After graduation I attended the Army

Truck Driving School (88M) at Fort Leonard Wood. During those years you could do what is called "on the job training" for other skills so I did that to become a field artilleryman. I spent time as an enlisted Soldier and rose to the rank of Staff Sergeant. At that time I went to Officer Candidate School and became a Second Lieutenant in the Military Police Corps. I spent time in the National Guard, the Army Reserve, and obviously, active duty Army: retiring with 37 years and 4 months of combined service.

During my time in service I've seen a lot of marriages fall apart in the Army. I have been told that the Army has the highest divorce rate of any organization in the world. By what

I witnessed, I believe it. I intend to help you keep your marriage and family together.

Chapter 1

Historical Failures of Men as Husbands, Fathers and Service Members

The true understanding of what leadership means in a Christian home is very valid. Leadership failures have made many men fall prey to their own selfish needs. I was that guy! What the scriptures in Ephesians are talking about is the responsibility for a family not political gains, not personal gain or military rank by any means.

There are many examples of great men who have failed by becoming selfish and giving in to their own desires.   One such example is King David, a commanding person in the Old Testament. He had an affair with one of his Soldier's wife. At the same time he was sending the Soldier into battle on the front lines and he lost his life in battle.

I could go on and on with a list of men that society has seen fail. Some of these highly visible men are Jimmy Swaggart, Bill Clinton, Jim Baker and even Saint Peter. If there is a silver lining to any man that has failed, that silver lining is that he learned from his failure and implemented change in his life. The big question is "how did those people find redemption"? In my own life I have found that the truthful answer to that question is admission, regret and learning. If we are only regretful that we got caught, it's not real. If you find regret burning in your heart of because of the action then you are more likely to improve and "start over".

I find my mind wandering back through my married life and something will pop up in my mind that makes me sick to my stomach. I remember once when we lived in Simpsonville, South Carolina and I was mobilized to Fort Jackson, South Carolina. Rhonda and I were separating (or I was) and she was planting flowers in the flower bed beside our driveway. Tears were streaming down her face as she continued to plant flowers and I was backing out of our driveway. That vision is one of many that will haunt me until my dying day! This was a very poor decision on my part! She has made her mistakes also but I don't think anyone has ever loved me like my wife has.

I was taking down that protectional fence in my marriage and of my family without even knowing what I was doing. The protection of the family is absolutely your responsibility! Whether you are physically home or not, you must always be thinking of your wife and kids protection and show them that you love them some how.

You can make it easy for your wife to lose interest in you by becoming passive and providing little to no attention to your family. Wives deserve your confidence, love, attention, protection, care, respect and concern in their lives day in and day out. Men can get lazy in these areas without even thinking about it as I am living proof. You get married, embark on career, have children and your focus tends to go to where the most noise comes from. Usually we will use the job as a reason that we are just tired or have little concern of doing family things.

I'll tell you another thing that we do and that is forget to thank the people in your life who have poured so much into you and your marriage over the years. We lived all over the United States and have had great neighbors and family members that showed us love and mentorship. I don't think I even recognized how much they were giving me as far as leadership until it may have been too late in some cases. My in-laws (Rodney and Dianne Beal) were always there when we had to make a move to ensure that we got settled into a new home. Little did I know how important that that was in our life. So much stress was relieved as we got settled in and started work at the new location. They sprinkled seeds of love around our life so many times that I couldn't begin to count. I only hope that they know how much we appreciate them even though I probably didn't show it very much.

We always had neighbors that would pitch in and watch the kids when we needed them to for appointments, rake the leaves in our yard and just always ready to lend a helping hand. I would always try to remember to say "thank you" but I'm not sure that I always returned the favor as a good man should. I know that I didn't recognize the energy they put into our family by just always keeping watch on us as well as helping out with any needs that we may have had. Some led us to their local church to keep that 3 legged stool (spiritual, mental and physical health) together. Me being what I thought was a man, would just take it for granted. Little did I know that God had put these people in my path and world to help me with goals which I didn't even know that I had yet. If you don't recognize that support from folks who pour love into your life, you are failing. And....if you don't take that lesson forward in your life and pour into someone else's life you are failing.

I have learned that there is no greater responsibility in my life than to ensure that our children are saved and understand the path of salvation. All of our (Rhonda and I) children are saved and are leading healthy lives of their own. This absolutely was a product of their mom and those same good people that God put in our life path. You see, you only have your kids for a little while on this earth while young and formidable. The formidable years are times that you influence them as parents. It's your opportunity to teach them about Christ and the plan of salvation because generally the world with teach them something else. At the end of life, you want to know that you will meet them again in heaven. I would like to take credit for the great parenting, but honestly I probably didn't provide enough care for the issue as a young father and dad.

<u>Chapter 2</u>

You are God's Hands!

What does it mean to be God's hands? I read a story one time about a family letting a child die without getting medical attention. All they were doing was praying and stating that God would take care of the child. Don't get confused about my thinking here. God can do anything! But remember God gave you a brain with a conscious to make decisions for your family. I always pray for an answer to problems and am not afraid to action on God's decisions nor to use the tools that He gives us.   I have executed what I thought was God's plan only to realize it was not in some cases. It was what I wanted God's plan to be. You must have that relationship and LISTEN very closely. It takes lots of practice and dedication to develop the walk with God that a family requires of a man. God doesn't give you a shovel to lean on and pray for a hole. Dig a hole with the tool that He gave you!

Also, don't forget about what we talked about in the last chapter about learning from folks investing in your family and carry that trait forward and invest in others. You will be glad that you did and will be God's hands in more ways than you understand.

Being a husband and a dad requires a purpose filled life not only for yourself but for the entire family. Everybody is your brother or sister on a bigger scale, but you have to lead your family in purposes that satisfy God and his plan of salvation. This purpose filled life will help your children to see an example of what being a Christian adult should look like. As a young family, we were able to spend time around my wife's grandparents table. This taught many things to our children about humility and being a family servant member. My in-laws were always interested in making others around them comfortable and happy. I have the greatest mother-in-law God ever made and to this day, she does everything possible to make those around her happy. My father in law always reminded us what time that church was on Sunday when we were there on a weekend visit. It wasn't a matter of IF we were going to church but you would be ready in time to make it to church. They are just more examples of strong mentorship from folks that God put in our path.

As a young married man for many years, I was living a self-centered life. I was more interested in gaining the next rank or doing something I thought was fun, when in reality I was missing some of the best opportunities to be a father and husband. I could have been God's hands in so many ways.

As of this writing I am in my 3rd year of reading the Bible from cover to cover. I am being led through this by another one of God's gifts of a good mentor.

I can't express to you enough of how I could have done much better as a husband and father had I spent more time on my knees praying and absorbing scripture as a young man.

As an old man who has lived long enough to learn, I have my quiet time every morning where I read my scripture and I pray for the protection of my family, friends, coworkers, world leaders and simply anyone that I think could use a little help from God. There is no better way to get time where you and God can talk. It's not a verbal voice that you will hear but consciously as you learn and listen, God will lead you.

I also found that hobbies with our kids were an exceptional way to keep them out of trouble and help them learn skills for life. Our girls were into swimming, gymnastics, track and those type things. They were really good at anything they set their mind to, just like in real life. The boys were into dirt track racing. It was probably my way of living vicariously through them as I did that as a kid also. The boys learned how to buy something and resale it for a profit. Basic life lessons of how to make and keep a dollar is important. They paid their way through college with scholarships, money saved and a job. I'm not the guy that believes that everyone needs a 4-year college degree but if you want it bad enough to pay for it then you work for it. Working for a college degree develops ownership and responsibility. This may sound ridiculous, but I think that my kiddos working and showing their friends the trait of responsibility was them being "God's Hands".

Being God's hands means holding your brother and sister accountable in life and expecting the same from them as well. This is not an easy task as we are all sinners and get put in a place of judgement by holding our brothers and sisters accountable. The discussions with your family and friends must be held with love. There is probably no quicker way to lose the opportunity than acting "over holy" in a corrective discussion. Also, be ready to receive more than you give others in corrections in accordance with God's Word. No matter how good that you think you are, you are not that good. Be humble.

Chapter 3

Head of Household

Head of Household doesn't mean you hold your chest out and act like you are the boss. Being the Head of the Household should be viewed as a descriptive term that explains and defines the role of servanthood within the family. The goal is not always to rule, but to relate on the level of needs in the life of your spouse and children, and to strive in meeting those needs and providing a sense of security. Looking back I think that I was a very lazy husband as far as contributions to leading the family. Rhonda was the one up with the kids, handling issues at school and keeping the family running day to day. I had that mindset that as long as I went to work and left her home with the kids that I was doing my part. Not so! If nothing more than integrating into the conversation of what was going on, I could have at least supported her thoughts and decisions. She strapped on her boots and ran the family every single time that I was weak. I owe a debt of gratitude for her and I thank God every day for salvaging our marriage. Men are stupid.

As a man is expected to lead, there are things that seem to be normal to us that will kill a marriage. Laziness as I mentioned earlier combined with a lack of respect for the job that your wife does. Motherhood is the hardest job in the world in my opinion. I think we men, play that role off and make them feel like they are lucky to not have to go to work everyday. Oh, they go to work and they are never allowed to call in sick or leave it in most cases. Other things that will kill a marriage are suspicion, lack of forgiveness, pointing out shortcomings of your wife and kids, and arguing. We should do everything possible to bring comfort to the wife and children when it comes to our own adulthood shortcomings.

Dads can't be a passive parent when children need discipline, and they can't leave mom hanging in this respect. Raising kids is hard work. You have to work together in the raising and disciplining of the kids. You don't want the world to discipline them. When that happens, it's too late.

If we men understood the real responsibility that God put on us, we would be having night sweats and panic attacks. Simply put, you are responsible for every wrong in the family while raising children and until you die. That sounds harsh huh? I don't like watching the news but spend a little time watching it for yourself and see the crime committed by kids. In your own mind, drill down into what caused the particular crime. I can think of a school shooting committed by a child in recent years. Was the child's anger from poor parenting that included too much social media and screen time? Was it from a broken home with no discipline? Was it from a lazy dad that didn't take the time to teach the kid certain things? I could go on and on, but I will tell you this. We have children being raised without the proper leadership in their life and it's paying negative dividends.

Here is something that I don't want you to miss. Your wife will make mistakes and you will be the first one to point it out in some case. Don't do this. If you spend more time trying to get yourself "right", the entire picture of your marriage will change for the better. Don't believe me? Try it for a week. Only focus on your shortcomings and fixing them. You will see and hopefully you focus more and more on your self daily to make improvements.

Always keep focused on social influence. There are so many influencers that it's almost impossible to protect your kids from. Let's make a quick list.

- Social media platforms that have very little oversight or protections for kid's little minds.

- 24 hour news channels that will talk about anything to keep the clock moving

- Kids and adults that have no morale background nor solid beliefs in anything.

- Disgruntled children at school that have a terrible homelife and are looking for someone weaker to bully in some cases.

- Teachers in public school that grew up without a solid foundation in Christ.

- School systems that make decisions off of the advisement of a board of directors that are politically charged.

We could go on and on with a list that contains, drugs, alcohol, etc but I think you get the point now. As a father, it is absolutely your job to make your kids understand right from wrong.

This is the point where I will tell you to let them fail. That's right, let them fail. It is better to learn how to respond to failure from the home rather than the public. Explain to them this whole concept that they will fail many times and you are teaching them to bounce back and be successful. Dust yourself off "kid"!

Chapter 4

Understand What Loving Your Wife Means

Husbands should love their wife as Christ loved the church and gave Himself up for her. This is an awesome responsibility that most of us can't or won't do because we don't understand the depth of Christ's love. If I may make a feeble attempt to dissect Christ's love, I would simply go to the cross. Christ died the most horrible death on the cross for our sins. Would you do that for your wife?

Have you prayed in front of your wife or with your wife for

answers? Will you stand confident with your wife that you are carrying out God's will or will you shy away from right and wrong decisions when it's not popular?

Most of us never even think of those things. We become infatuated with a girl, get married and see how it goes. I think it's because we don't integrate God into our lives from the beginning. We do not reach out to or bring God into our marriage until we get into trouble or have a problem. It really should be the opposite, and this leads to the importance of having a good understanding of the husband's role before you get married. The woman that you marry deserves to have the very best example of masculinity, confidence, good decision making, action man even when he is scared to take care of his family and many more things. Lust will wear off with time and you are given the responsibility for developing a platform on which to build a family with the greatest amount of support to your wife.

Marriage counseling is a wonderful thing. That's right, I said it and mean it. Whenever we had to go to counseling, I didn't think it was all that cool. I am a grown man and don't need any help… or at least that's what I thought. Our kids even went to counseling some. I am internally sad about that because I wasn't doing what I should have been doing in my marriage as a father and man.

One time when Rhonda and I went to counseling with a pastor of ours (John Robbins), he asked us the question "Who do you love more, your spouse or your kids"? Without hesitation we both said that we loved our kids more. What he helped us to understand is that if you love your kids, you have to love your spouse that you made the kids with more. Why? The kids are in a precarious situation when asked to choose or feel love from one parent more than the other. At some point you loved your spouse enough to engage in the development of a life. You and your wife have developed a baby! That child is dependent upon you for life in my opinion. Why would it be right to say that you love the kids but don't love the person that loved you enough to give you a child? Honestly, red lights started flashing for me personally. I still do things that don't make my wife happy I'm sure, but I consciously try to show her that I love her and would give my life for her in a second. No questions asked!

What I would ask you to do in your marriage concerning the

love for your wife is to consciously try to think before you speak harsh words because you can never take those back. Show her that you love her through your actions. I'm not saying that you have to buy flowers or cards for every little thing but support her in anything that she needs from you. She needs your support. She will have squabbles with her family and friends, she will get negatively judged by people, she will burn supper, she will second guess herself and many other things will come at her in life. Do you know whose job that is to "catch her"? Yours! Simply praying for her daily and standing solidly beside her as she needs help in making a decision. Here is you another big thing. You will need her more that she will need you but you just don't know it.

That part in Ephesians about leaving your mother and father to be united with your wife is so important. Not sure when I finally got that but as I look back I see times when I let my wife's needs down to cater to my family. I see this in a lot of young marriages. It doesn't mean that you forget your parents or not help them out. It means that your primary focus in marriage is your wife. If you are certain to make your marriage work there is no room for negotiating around your wife's needs. I know that there are situations where your wife may just be jealous of your relationship with your mom and she is always looking for reasons to inject into that relationship. That's another issue that you will need to work through. But with all things being equal, your world, calendar, resources, etc., go into your wife and family. We've all seen the "mother-in-law" issues that sometimes rear their head for "mama's boy". Your job is to smooth that out as the husband and it doesn't mean that you fail your wife. It's hard math but a problem that must be resolved. You can't cut ties with your mom and you can't cut ties with your wife, but if you don't constantly work it, one of them will cut the tie for you.

I believe one of my shortfalls was in my own confidence level as Rhonda's husband. She is just so much smarter than me on so many levels and it was evident early on in our marriage. I would have trouble finding a decision and in reality left her to make the decision. Many examples come to mind to include finances. You know money is one of those things that young couples argue about a lot. I was a bit looser with money than she was. I wouldn't hesitate to buy a motorcycle or something I wanted or thought that I needed when she was clipping coupons to ensure that we could buy groceries. What's the decision you ask? The decision was whether we were conservative and saved some money or not. This one is a big thing that you need to start early with. She was able to save us enough money for her to stay home and raise our kids. You can't replace good child rearing with any amount of money.

There are a ton of decisions to be made but talking about them together will make it easier with less fights. Where are we going to church? What are we going to do about the car when it's broke down? Can we afford something? If you don't help make decisions, your force her to do it and then you get upset in some cases!

That confidence level is a "learned attribute" where a man must be willing to swallow his pride and learn in order to achieve it.

There are many organizations that your wife can become a part of that will help her when / if you are deployed. Most units have a family readiness group and a spouses club. Ensure that you link your wife in to these as many have a lot of experience that will help to solve a lot of family issues such as childcare, job information and marital support just to name a few.

Normally when I saw a Soldier that didn't want to involve his wife, there were motives that weren't good. He can't cheat on his wife if folks know who she is and have friendships with her.

To have greater odds of being successful at anything especially your marriage. Your wife will likely need the friendships of the organizations for spouses. When you are gone to training or combat, she will need her new found friends to lean on.

My wife has made lifelong friends along the way just as I have. The support from those friends comes in many different ways.

Not every wife wants to be a part of these things but you must expose her to these things and let her make the choice. My wife found these opportunities fulfilling, especially when she had the opportunity to help another Soldier's family.

As a young man we don't like hearing our wife call their name as it is normally includes a task to be completed. When you get older, you will be grateful that someone loves you and believes in you enough to call your name instead of someone else.

Chapter 5

Loving Your Children

Have your kids seen you pray? I'm not talking about a quick blessing over a meal. I mean really seen you pray? Children are like magnets and will emulate what they see. Our children learned to say their nightly prayers at a very young age and we would sometimes mention to them to pray for their friends or something simple that would help someone's life. It was probably more symbolic for them to gain an understanding to remember to pray for others. I'm not sure that my children have seen me pray earnestly for forgiveness or help but I sure have as a dad.

I spend every morning praying for my family and others as well. I mentioned praying in passing with my kids when we ran into a questionable situation no matter what it was. I tried to make that my "first call" when a questionable situation arose in front of them on purpose.

Discipline was something in our house that our kids understood. They understood that discipline was a viable "thing" when they did not listen. We never "beat" our kids out of anger or anything silly like that. I think that Rhonda and I both were so afraid of the world disciplining our kids if we didn't and we knew that that wouldn't go good. I can still see the tears in the eyes of our kids to this day but I can assure you that they understand Jesus Christ, accountability, responsibility and treating others as you would want to be treated. They will thrive and survive!

As discussed before, we found things to do with our kids as they grew to spend time with them. Were they always the right things? I don't know. Our girls liked gymnastics, track and swimming. The boys were a little easier for me as they took up with dirt track racing like I did as a kid. Yeah, there were sometimes at the track foul language and alcohol, but that family of racers would do anything for you. They learned so many things with these hobbies and building relationships over time. Our kids are the greatest if you ask me. Yeah, I'm a little bit biased but I am mighty proud of them.

Tanner, our oldest son went to

counseling one time and he was asked

the question "What would you do if

your mom and dad weren't around?"
His answer was that he would hook his wagon to his bicycle and take his siblings to his grandparents' house. I can tell you that it was a gut punch for me for my kids to even be in this situation. It also showed me a sign of how resilient our kids are.

Again, they should never have been in a situation like this, but life happens and if your child needs counseling, get them counseling. What we men don't do, is consider the effects on our kids when we have disputes with our wives. PTSD is a real thing and I think we men can be held consciously responsible for our children having PTSD. So if you give a damn about your kids, think before you act and then....think again.

In this world there is evil and danger around every corner of children's lives. We taught our children how to use a gun and be safe with it and respect it. We taught them about misuse of alcohol, and drugs, the safety and rules of riding motorcycles, and other things that came into their lives. They must know how to deal with life matters and know what to do when they fail. We let our children fail when the opportunity arose only to teach them how to get up and dust themselves off and keep moving forward.

Social media seems to be a babysitter these days in some cases. What goes into the brain will shape a child's thought process and I can tell you that most of what they are seeing is not good. Too much screen time has many negative effects on the shaping of a child's demeanor and perception of the real world. Have them get involved with hands-on type of hobbies and spend time teaching them about the real world. Kids are like magnets and will attach themselves to things that they shouldn't if you don't teach them what they should attach themselves to.

One of the greatest benefits of the military service, in our case the Army, was the exposure to so many good people and places. Our children played sports at so many different locations and levels, made lifelong friends that they have kept in touch with and also were exposed to so many different cultures.

Yes, there were always those sad times when they had to say goodbye to friends as we were told to move to a different location for the

Army. Even through these hard times I believe that they learned resilience.

Culture was a big one. Our children learned that all people are good in most cases. No skin color ever made a difference to our children. The ranks of their friends' parents were never an issue. They loved their friends as well as their friends' families.

The Army came up with this interpreter / translator program which I had the opportunity to command. These folks were from different parts of the Middle East. They were students to me but in years afterwards some became friends and taught our children so many things about what their culture, beliefs, and life was like as a child growing up in a third world country. When we visited each other's families, they would provide food from their culture and our kids learned to like more than macaroni and cheese. I would go deeper on this subject and say that when our kids see something on the news about those countries they have learned about and have a connection with that they have a stronger acceptance and understanding of what is really happening.

Chapter 6
The Greatest
Responsibility

The greatest responsibility (Family Spiritual Heritage) within your household is to ensure that every member of your family is saved by the grace of God. Knowing that you will all link up in Heaven is the most important achievement of your life.

You need to set the example way earlier in life than I did. I reach back to my thoughts of my father-in-law and how there was an expectation that we were ready for church and made it on time. I learned so much from him and how he carried himself. He never really told me in words what his expectations were but he showed me with actions in real life. Our children watched him as well and as understood that as child of God you have requirements of learning. In other words, if you want to be a good Christian or human being then you needed to practice.

I also must commend my wife for finding a church for us to integrate into as we moved from duty station to duty station. We would develop friendships at church which would be followed by friendships for our children. If you compare that type of friendship to one of only worldly friendships, your children will turn out totally different. You can look around and see the difference in how they turned out.

Chapter 7
Have the Right People in Your Path

Ask God to put people (Relationships/Community Building) in your path to make you stronger. Take the initiative to surround yourself with the right people, which will mean having the proper boundaries to ensure the wrong people will not have space to initiate a negative influence.

The right people will have a heart and mind focused on pleasing God. They will also be the people who are willing to speak truth into your own heart and mind and will be intent in helping you be a disciple, or student, of Jesus Christ. This is a follow on to the discussion in a previous chapter about having the right people in your life. I think that we were blessed to have the right people at the right time placed into our lives. This is true of neighbors at the different duty stations and homes we lived in.

One such neighbor was Bob Hubble who lived beside of us in Columbia, South Carolina with his wife Mary. They were always inviting us for dinner and would play individually with our kids. Just another outpouring of love. Bob is probably one of those people that I didn't know that I needed but God did. I realize now that I needed him. His father was a retired Army Colonel and I enjoyed talking and learning from him. If Bob or his family ever said a bad thing about anyone, I never heard it. They invited us to Shandon Baptist Church where they attended and it was a great place for us. We would go eat dinner on Wednesday nights and have some good conversations that educated a young dad like me. Even after we moved and even now, Bob called and continues to call to check on us and how the kids are doing. Two of our kids went to college at the University of South Carolina and guess who was there to invite them to church when we didn't have eyes on them? That's right, Bob was still working to make my family successful.

Chapter 8
Your Leaders

Your leaders are currently under stress from above and below so be understanding when they get it wrong sometimes. In a lot of cases, they have stressors at home as well with a wife and/or children.

Your job is to make them successful which in turn makes the entire unit successful which could mean life or death in a combat zone.

By the time that you reach your first unit, you start to understand what Basic Training was all about and why they did some of the things that they did to you. While you were going through it, you thought that they were trying to break you down when in reality they were developing your mental agility. This mental agility will serve you well in making decisions when your boss isn't there.

Mentorship by the right person will pay you great dividends. I have many folks that come to memory from over the years that invested in me. Mentorship is not normally something written down that forces someone to mentor you. You will know when you find that person and you will naturally follow them. They will be a transparent and honest person that always completes the mission while putting their Soldiers first. The Soldiers will also receive the credit as a good mentor does not normally look for the limelight.

Chapter 9
Your Subordinates

You remember what it was like to be the new guy right? When I was a young Soldier, it seemed like all they wanted me to do was carry heavy rounds for a 155 Self-propelled Howitzer from one place to another. Little did I know that I was learning more about field artillery each day because they came to trust me. The trust for me doing the simple jobs led to them teaching me more of the "fun stuff," like yanking the cord that would send that 155-round barreling towards a target that I would never see but I knew that we were causing significant damage to that target.

If you hang around long enough, you will have folks who not only report to you but trust you to lead them through some very difficult tasks. Always be transparent in your orders and take the time to explain as much as possible, especially in the beginning. Trust must run both ways and if you ever fail them, they will see you in a way that you will not like. You will sometimes receive orders for distribution to your subordinates that you don't understand. You owe it to them to gather as much information as possible and if you can't, just be honest. Don't be honest in a negative way that would demean your leaders. Again, that will develop into a mistrust with your subordinate to an even higher level than you.

I worked for an NCO one time that was so negative of the command that I wasn't sure why they kept him around. He would receive orders that he didn't understand the "why" and wouldn't take the time to gather more information. We all know that he had time in the Operations meeting to ask questions but just failed to. He would come out to the formation with what he had and blame the leadership for such low amounts of information. This was in front of a platoon of Soldiers. Morale tanked!

After a while of this, some of the squad leaders got tired of coming up short on simple missions as well as losing credibility from their Soldiers. They actually began to huddle after the daily receipt of missions and forced the platoon sergeant to help them get more information. This helped morale out a lot and believe it or not, the platoon sergeant started gathering more information so as not to be seen as a low performer.

I learned early on not to be a lazy leader or at least I tried not to be because I knew what it was like to work for someone like that.

If you want to keep good Soldiers, you have to constantly think of their needs as well and when we are young we have lots of needs whether real or not. It takes time to help a young Soldier grow and understand where they fit into the big picture.

Chapter 10
Your Peers

Peers are awesome if you pick the right ones. A good rule of thumb is, if you are married, have peers that are married. Introduce the wives to each other to allow your wife to develop friendships with your peer's family. Having peers that are single is an option as long as it don't turn into a drinking buddy that you hang out with and leave your wife and family at home.

I would also recommend to not find the love of your life in a peer group within your unit. Very few of these actually make it and it'll just turn out to be drama when it falls apart.

Another great benefit for making friends with couples is that if you both have children, they have the opportunity to develop a friendship that may last a lifetime.

Peers must always be honest with each other as well. Be willing to listen and give good solid advice. A true peer / friend will always be honest.

Chapter 11
Additional Resources

There is a following chapter about using your Chaplain and some of the resources they can provide but lets start with the ultimate tool that they can provide you with, the Bible. You, as a man must educate yourself in a lot of things but nothing more important than the Bible. When people say that there is no book on how to be a husband or father, they are wrong. I'm not asking you to become some holy roller, but you have to know the rules of the highway, so start small. Pick a time of day when you can have quiet time and dig in. There are apps out there that will lead you through the Bible without stressing you out. As I said earlier, I'm in my third year of reading it all the way through and I see so many things that I missed last year. It's ok. Make time for it.

The following is not an entire list but lots of great resources for a military family. Generally, you can Google these combined with your post or duty station to find a contact number locally.

- MWR (Morale, Welfare and Recreation) provides many different programs to support families from financial issues consisting of grants and zero interest loans to helping the spouse find a job at a new duty station. Childcare providers either on post or off post in some cases is a priority for

MWR so you can focus on the force. Reach out to find your local organization at https://www.armymwr.com .

- Unit Family Readiness Groups (FRG) – Not all units have an FRG but if they do, ensure to introduce your wife to the FRG leader and let her choose if she wants to get involved. Rhonda has made so many friends in these organizations, not to mention supporting other families as needed. There is normally an email distro when you get to a unit to make contact with the FRG leader.

- National Suicide Crisis Line – 988 – Never hesitate to make the call and talk to someone. You will not be judged, and a full network of support will help you. We all need help at some point and I hope you learn that its not shameful to ask for help.

- Military OneSource-Provides confidential counseling and a list of other things that may be needed at no cost to families. Reach out to https://www.militaryonesource.mil to find your local contact. Google is always a friend to find local also.

- United Service Organization (USO) -I have found this organization very user friendly especially when the service member is deployed. They physically set up in areas where service members go to fight. Reach out to their page for questions at https://www.uso.org for any questions or support.

- Army Emergency Relief (AER) – Every post, base or station has this organization or a representative to link you into the support that you need. https://www.armyemergencyrelief.org

AER has always been a great starting point for financial issues as they arrive in your young military family life.

Chapter 12
Use Your Chaplain

Chaplains can be your greatest friends and a source of support as I am living proof of that. I have some dear Chaplain friends to this day. COL (R) Cliff Vicars is one of my dearest friends and is also a contributor to this book.

Many years have passed since I went to Officer Candidate School, and I have forgotten more than I have learned but I will always remember Chaplain Hales who was assigned to our OCS cohort / class. We would come back to the barracks at night with bloody hands and knees only to find him waiting to just listen to us. He knew the game or process of Officer Candidate School I'm sure, but he never acted like we should be stronger. He never belittled us or made us feel weak. He instead listened to our worries and problems and then would provide us some scripture to bring us some sort of peace or to ease the pain. He would always ask if we had the chance to talk to our loved ones, if we needed special prayer for someone we loved and sometimes he would bring in some snacks to us. I'm pretty sure that he wasn't supposed to do that but we knew he loved and cared about us.

Sometime later in life I was a Company Commander for a basic training unit at Fort Jackson, South Carolina and I met our Battalion Chaplain, Cliff Vicars. We hit it off from day one. Not only did he counsel me on my own personal issues, but he had and still has a deep love for Soldiers. When I had Soldiers that wanted to go to behavioral health appointments, I would always send them to Cliff first. Chaplains can have conversations that no one will ever know about and have a way of bringing peace to a scared trainee. These trainees were never told that they couldn't go to behavioral health but some large number didn't need to go after talking with Cliff. Most had family issues or adaptation issues which were overwhelming, and Cliff added them to his list to keep an eye on like they were his children. They were able to return to training and became graduates of Basic Combat Training.

For my own personal issues such as my marriage, Cliff stepped in and made sure that I could share with him and function as a Commander. I did a lot of listening to this man.

He not only did marriage counseling for Rhonda and I but he

also drove to my home town when my daddy passed away and did his funeral. This last year he also performed the wedding for my daughter and her husband. He is family for life.

Chapter 13
Money!??

I won't profess to teach you how to handle the money other than let your wife do it in most cases. Mr. Man, you may have an accounting brain but I don't and many of us don't.

Separate checking and savings accounts are a bad idea and I will tell you that it is a sign of not being committed to the relationship in my opinion. As a man and woman come together to be as one, so should the resources. Generally, there is nothing that you will argue about more than the money. One of the reasons is as a young couple you don't have much money in the first place.

Put your pride away and be open about money. No secret credit cards, no secret stash, and again, no secret accounts at all. The quicker that you learn to be honest and discuss the money, it'll work out better.

Use the same energy into determining how to get and keep more money in the family. I think that I've had a side business almost my entire career but the key is that you do it together. We've owned a Chimney sweep business, a bar, a trucking company, a security company and a pool business. Having a business or side job is hard to do and you must get approval from your chain of command. It worked out for us over the years. In another book I'll help folks understand how to do side business for a retirement cushion.

Don't be afraid to cut grass or wash other folks' cars on the weekends to make extra money. We have a little bit of "mattress money" that has saved us from being broke before.

Both of you have access to the mattress money and both of you can earn the money to put in there. You both have some kind of skills that you can use to add to this little pot of gold.

As with any of the other money, talk about what goes in and what comes out. Keep a paper in the stash to record what you take out and put in.

Chapter 14
Near the End

Now that I am retired, I feel like I'm on the airplane ride of life and the Captain has come over the intercom to tell us that we are starting our descent. He tells us "Ladies and Gentlemen we have started our descent, and we will have you on the ground in about 30 minutes". This tells me that I must be buckled up for safety and get rid of my trash in my life. I've been more blessed than most by my Lord and Savior in this life but I feel sometimes like I'm lacking in many ways. Have I done everything for my "landing" of life?

Some may take that as a negative view but honestly, I feel fortunate to have lived through the experiences I have had and completed the journeys before me. The end is inevitable for your childhood, school, time on station, your career and life so make the best of everyday. Make sure that you make amends with people everyday. Ask for forgiveness to anyone that you may have harmed. You owe it to them and yourself. Jesus expects it from you as the leader of the family.

I hope that you as the reader will chase your dreams with a family like mine. You will fail many times in most things that you try but that is how you learn. Break into your dreams with zeal and a positive attitude, when you fail get up and try it again until you succeed. Nobody controls your destiny but you!

A couple things to leave you with to help you be successful.

Who is your Chaplain?

_____

What is his/her phone number?

_____

What is the website for the Family Readiness Group?

_____

Did you share with your wife?

_____

Is there a Spouse's Club and do you have contact info?

_____

Does your wife have the info and have you introduced them?

_____

_____

About The Author

Chris is an Author, a veteran of the US Army, a business man and a strong advocate to supporting service members coming along behind him. Over his more than 37 years of service in the Army he has worked both as an enlisted member and a commissioned officer.

These positions helped him gain an understanding of many different situations that let him work to develop the best in others. One of the biggest lessons learned was that you truly have to be a follower to understand how to lead.

Chris hails from Maiden, North Carolina and is a combat Veteran of the United States Army. As an enlisted member. he served in the Field Artillery branch, achieving the rank of Staff Sergeant. He later attended Officer Candidate School, where he branched with the Military Police Corps. He has held many positions that normally Military Policemen don't get to work in. The best example of this is that he spent the last five years of his career working with Joint Task Force North working counter drug organizations and the Southern border mission.

Early in his career he spent time in the National Guard and the United States Army Reserve. During this time he worked for BMW as Lean Six Sigma Black Belt. This is where is learned the most about project management and developing teams with folks that had much more expertise in the auto industry. He has also had businesses along the way throughout his career to include a bar, a security company and a pool business.

Chris has sat on many boards for organizations that he believes in that support not only service members but humanity in general. He has sat on the USO board and, at the time of this book's publication, the board for the El Paso Rescue Mission. The El Paso Rescue Mission provides a program to help people with alcohol and drug addiction to leave that life and never return. This program includes housing and coursework while also learning a skill by working in the restaurant business. Hallelujah BBQ is a sister non-profit to educate students in the industry while providing support to the organization.

Chris holds a Bachelors of Business Administration and a Masters of Business and Organizational Security Management.

His most treasured accomplishments are his family with 35 years of marriage, at the time of this book's publication in 2025, and serving in the military for over 37 years.

Chris enjoys hearing from readers. You can contact him / give him feedback by emailing him at cwoody@yourpatriotentertainment.com. If you would like to review this book please leave a review on Barnes and Noble, Walmart, Amazon or other retailer pages.

You can keep up with Chris's projects by going to his company's website www.yourpatriotentertainment.com.

www.ingramcontent.com/pod-product-compliance
Lightning Source LLC
Chambersburg PA
CBHW051217120626
46547CB00013B/1387